GW01159201

Original title:
Architectural Rhythms

Author: Clement Portlander
ISBN HARDBACK: 978-9916-88-068-5
ISBN PAPERBACK: 978-9916-88-069-2

The Flow of Façades

Windows gleam in the sun's soft light,
Patterns dance in the fading night.
Brick by brick, stories unfold,
Echoes of dreams, both new and old.

Colors clash in vibrant play,
Whispers of life in every sway.
Balconies greet the summer breeze,
A harmony of art that frees.

Textures of Tranquility

Pebbles crunch beneath my feet,
Nature's rhythm, calm and sweet.
The gentle rustle of the trees,
A soothing balm, a quiet ease.

Soft shadows dance on the ground,
In the stillness, peace is found.
Mossy stones and lichen's grace,
In this haven, time finds space.

Shadows of Structure

Morning light breaks, the skyline wakes,
Silhouettes stir as the world stakes.
Bold outlines claim the open sky,
In framed shadows, ambitions lie.

Shapes emerge in a fluid form,
A testament to the norm.
Each corner tells a hidden tale,
In architecture, dreams prevail.

The Fabric of Buildings

Walls woven with sweat and stone,
Every creak a whispered tone.
Steel and glass in sleek embrace,
In every structure, a sacred space.

From foundation to rooftop's kiss,
Each design holds a piece of bliss.
Life and time intertwine and blend,
In the fabric of buildings, we depend.

Symmetry in Shadows

In twilight's hush, the forms align,
Echoes cast in dark design.
Every angle, sharp and clear,
Whispers tell what we both fear.

Branches stretch, a silent reach,
Lessons learned that time will teach.
In the stillness, secrets blend,
Nature's art that will not end.

Lines of Life

Paths diverge in morning light,
Choices made in gentle flight.
Every step, a tale unfolds,
In the warmth, the truth beholds.

Twists and turns, we navigate,
Lessons found, we elevate.
Through the storms and sunny days,
Life's a canvas, we portray.

The Dance of Foundations

Underneath the stones we place,
Roots entwined in nature's grace.
Every layer tells a tale,
History's breaths in each detail.

From the ground, we rise and sway,
Holding strong as skies turn grey.
In unity, our spirits soar,
Building dreams, forevermore.

Urban Cadence

City beats, a pulse so bright,
Life ignites in neon light.
Every block, a story wakes,
In the rhythm, the heart breaks.

Footsteps echo, hopes collide,
In the chaos, dreams abide.
As the skyline fades to night,
Voices blend in muted light.

Melodies of Masonry

Chiseled stones in morning light,
Each brick holds dreams in its sight.
Whispers of hands, a craft divine,
In every seam, a story aligns.

Echoes of hammers, a rhythmic beat,
Harmony where earth and sky meet.
Beneath the arches, shadows play,
Masonry sings in a timeless way.

The Dance of Dimensions

Shapes intertwine in a graceful flow,
Curves and angles, a vibrant show.
Each line extends, a story unfolds,
In space and time, bold dreams are told.

Steps of a journey, soft and slow,
Framing the world in colors aglow.
Dimensions whisper, while shadows prance,
Unity found in the dance of chance.

Symmetry in Stillness

Silence reigns in perfect form,
Nature's balance, a soothing norm.
Through quiet spaces, peace is found,
In every corner, beauty is bound.

Mirrored visions in tranquil sight,
Reflections dance in the soft twilight.
Geometry of life, poised and neat,
In stillness, all the world feels complete.

Lyrical Landscapes

Mountains rise in poetic grace,
Valleys cradle, a warm embrace.
Rivers flow with melodious ease,
Nature's song among the trees.

Sunset paints the twilight hue,
Whispers carried on winds anew.
In every leaf and every stone,
Lyrical landscapes call us home.

Foundations of Reflection

In silence pools, where dreams reside,
Mirrors capture the heart's tide.
Each thought a ripple, softly flows,
Anchored deep where the stillness grows.

Beneath the surface, secrets hide,
Whispers echo, dreams confide.
Time stands still in this gentle place,
Finding peace in the mirrored space.

Crescendo of Arches

Under arches, voices soar,
Harmonies rise, forevermore.
Each step forward, a tale unfolds,
In the heartbeat of stone, secrets told.

Sunlight dances on ancient walls,
Echoes linger as nightfall calls.
The journey bends, a symphony,
In the arches, we find unity.

The Pulse of Facades

Facades gleam in the twilight glow,
Life pulses beneath, though few may know.
Windows echo the stories they keep,
Behind each layer, the city sleeps.

Colors shift as shadows play,
The rhythm of life in a silent sway.
Every corner, a breath to take,
The pulse of facades, a heartbeat awake.

Tapestry of Shadows

In the weave of night, shadows blend,
Patterns form as colors suspend.
Each thread whispers tales of old,
A tapestry of dreams to behold.

With every flicker, the darkness sings,
Stories carried on silent wings.
In shadow's embrace, we all belong,
A dance of light, a heartbeat song.

Cadence of Corners

In the stillness found at dusk,
Corners whisper tales of old,
Fragments of laughter and rust,
Time's gentle touch, stories told.

The wind stirs softly through eaves,
Each turn a secret it keeps,
With shadows that dance in leaves,
As the world quietly sleeps.

Bright sun spills over the bricks,
Adding warmth to worn-out dreams,
Every angle, stories predict,
Life flows like a stream of beams.

A mosaic of moments gone,
In each space, a heartbeat thrives,
Corners that gaze at the dawn,
Where the past and future jive.

The Symphony of Space

In the silence of the night,
Stars hum a cosmic tune,
Galaxies whirl in delight,
Beneath a watching moon.

Each planet spins its own song,
Harmonies drift through the breeze,
Echoes of where we belong,
Twinkling in cosmic seas.

Waves crash on distant shores,
Resonating with the stars,
Nature plays through open doors,
A melody that's ours.

In this vast, unending space,
We are notes in the design,
Finding beauty's warm embrace,
In this symphony divine.

Shadows on the Facade

As daylight fades to twilight's grace,
Shadows stretch, a silent dance,
Every wall, a new embrace,
Whispers weave through chance.

Painting stories on the stone,
Mysteries tucked behind closed eyes,
Each shadow carves its own tone,
Underneath the twilight skies.

A facade wears the dusk's attire,
Flickers of ghosts in the light,
With secrets that never tire,
Fading softly into night.

Old structures sigh as shadows play,
Their tales etched in every fold,
Before the sun forgets to stay,
While the stars turn dreams to gold.

A Gathering of Forms

Shapes collide in muted light,
Figures twist in gentle flow,
A dance of shadows, bright and slight,
Where the wild spirits go.

Lines converge in playful beams,
Curves embrace the air they wind,
In this realm, nothing's as it seems,
Forming worlds both brave and kind.

Each angle tells a story new,
Triangles pulse with vibrant hue,
Circles spiral in rhythmic cue,
Inviting us to see it through.

Together crafting a sweet song,
A harmony without refrain,
In the heart where we belong,
A gathering, free from pain.

Resonance of Windows

Windows open to the sky,
Whispers of the world go by.
Light dances on the floor,
Echoes of dreams implore.

Framed views of life unfold,
Stories waiting to be told.
The glass reflects our gaze,
Capturing fleeting rays.

Shadows play with soft delight,
Fragments of day turn to night.
Through each pane, a view remains,
Silent beauty, joy, and pains.

In the stillness, truths arise,
Resonance in the skies.
A moment caught in time,
Windows hold life sublime.

The Fabric of Form

Threads weave through the breath of night,
Shapes emerge in soft twilight.
Patterns dance on fabric's skin,
A world where all can spin.

Each curve tells a story grand,
Crafted by a mindful hand.
Textures whisper into sound,
In this space, dreams abound.

Forms arise from silent thoughts,
Knotted truths and tangled knots.
In every fold, a tale is spun,
A journey shared by everyone.

The fabric of our lives combined,
In colors rich, the heart aligned.
Through art, we shape our way,
In form, we find our play.

Poetry in Proportions

Lines measured in gentle grace,
Words find their rightful place.
Rhythms pulse and softly speak,
In each stanza, beauty's peak.

Echoes of a structured thought,
Harmony from what is sought.
In each metaphor we weave,
The heart learns how to believe.

Verses grow with tender care,
Shaping moments rich and rare.
Proportions guide the steady hand,
Creating worlds where dreams can stand.

In the cadence, life unfolds,
Stories held in hearts' strong holds.
Poetry, a crafted art,
With proportions, we take part.

The Heartbeat of Hardscape

Concrete's pulse beneath our feet,
Streets hum with urban beat.
Buildings rise like steadfast dreams,
In their shadows, sunlight beams.

Brick and stone, a tale is laid,
Structures strong, yet softly swayed.
Pavements tell of journeys tread,
In each crack, a path is spread.

Metal frames reach toward the skies,
Holding whispers, silent cries.
Yet in this hardness, life does thrive,
A heartbeat found where we arrive.

Nature meets with artistry,
In hardscapes, endless mystery.
Balance struck in grit and grace,
Awakens life in every space.

Layers of Light

Soft whispers hang in the air,
Golden beams in a gentle stare.
Color dances through the trees,
Painting shadows with such ease.

Morning breaks with tender grace,
Illuminating every place.
Nature's canvas glows so bright,
Embraced in layers of pure light.

Evening falls with a warm hue,
The world wrapped in twilight's view.
Stars emerge in a velvet sky,
Guiding dreams as they drift by.

The Pulse of Pathways

Footsteps echo on the ground,
A heartbeat whispered, all around.
Each path leads to tales untold,
Secrets shared, and dreams unfold.

Beneath the arch of ancient trees,
Rustling leaves dance with the breeze.
Every corner a new delight,
A journey woven with pure light.

Rivers flow, a steady guide,
Carrying thoughts with the tide.
In the rhythm of night and day,
The pulse of pathways finds its way.

Towers in Twilight

Tall structures scrape the evening sky,
Bathed in amber, the world sighs.
Shadows stretch and softly blend,
As day gives way, and night descends.

The city breathes, a vibrant song,
Where dreams and hopes together throng.
Each window tells a tale to keep,
Guardians of secrets in silence deep.

Whispers rise on the evening air,
Stories woven in threads of care.
As stars flicker, the towers stand,
Sentinels of this timeless land.

Dance of the Domes

In the sky, the domes align,
Promising magic, pure, divine.
They sway with grace, a cosmic dance,
Inviting hearts to take a chance.

Colors swirl in a cosmic breeze,
A gentle touch, as time agrees.
Each dome a note in harmony,
Resonating with eternity.

Underneath, the world spins bright,
In that glow, all fears take flight.
As the dance unfolds, hearts entwine,
With every pulse, the stars align.

The Balance of Grace

In whispers soft, the seasons blend,
A dance of light, where shadows bend.
Each step a trace of life's embrace,
In every heart, the balance of grace.

The stars alight, a hopeful theme,
As dreams are born from starlit beams.
With every tear, a smile we face,
In every soul, the balance of grace.

Through trials faced and paths we roam,
We find the strength to call it home.
In love's sweet warmth, we find our place,
In every heart, the balance of grace.

And when the night seems dark and long,
We'll sing our truths, a unified song.
For in the dawn, we find our pace,
In every soul, the balance of grace.

Tones of Terra

The earth beneath, a rhythmic pulse,
In colors bright, nature convulse.
Each gust of wind, a soft caress,
In every note, the tones of terra.

Mountains rise with stories old,
In their shadows, secrets told.
Rivers flow, a timeless quest,
In every drop, the tones of terra.

Through fields of gold and skies so wide,
In every heart, the world's pride.
A symphony in every breath,
In every sound, the tones of terra.

As seasons change, the canvas sways,
In nature's song, we find our ways.
With every step, we are blessed,
In every heart, the tones of terra.

Mosaic Melodies

Each piece a story, colors collide,
In harmony, we will abide.
Fragments dance, a vibrant embrace,
In every heart, mosaic melodies.

The laughter shared, a joyous sound,
In unity, our hopes are found.
Dreams intertwine in every space,
In every soul, mosaic melodies.

Voices rise, a sweet refrain,
Through joy and sorrow, love will reign.
With every chord, we find our grace,
In every heart, mosaic melodies.

Together we weave the tapestry bright,
In every stitch, the warmth of light.
As one we stand, in life's embrace,
In every soul, mosaic melodies.

Foundations of Flight

From earth we rise, on wings of dreams,
Through endless skies, life gently beams.
With hopes alight, we soar the height,
In every heart, foundations of flight.

The winds will guide, our spirits free,
Through realms unknown, our destiny.
With courage bold, we'll navigate,
In every soul, foundations of flight.

The clouds below, a canvas vast,
Each journey taken, shadows cast.
With every leap, we celebrate,
In every heart, foundations of flight.

As stars align in midnight's glow,
We'll chase the dreams that ebb and flow.
With every breath, we navigate,
In every soul, foundations of flight.

Resonance in Rebar

Iron veins in concrete flow,
Echoes of strength in a silent show.
Foundations holding dreams and fears,
Through storms and time, it perseveres.

Rigid rods beneath the skin,
Sustaining life, where we begin.
A heartbeat thumps in every layer,
Resonance found in the quiet prayer.

Rust may claim its glinting grace,
Yet still, it stands—a solid trace.
Crafted by hands that shaped the clay,
A legacy bold that won't decay.

In the shadows, steel will gleam,
Holding hopes, weaving dreams.
Through labor's sweat, and vision's spark,
The city's echo in the dark.

The Heartbeat of Habitats

Beneath the leaves, the whispers flow,
Life awakens, gentle and slow.
Roots intertwine in rich embrace,
A symphony found in nature's grace.

Wings flutter, calls rise and fall,
Echoing stories that weave through all.
The pulse of earth in every beat,
Each creature's rhythm, a dance so sweet.

Rivers carve paths through stone and grain,
Reflecting sunlight, embracing rain.
In tangled forests, secrets hide,
The heartbeat of habitats, wide and wild.

From hills to shores, the cycle spins,
In every end, a new life begins.
An everlasting tale unfolds,
Of worlds created, wonders untold.

Silvery Skylines

In twilight hues, the city gleams,
Mirroring aspirations and dreams.
Steel and glass, they twist and rise,
Engulfing clouds in expansive skies.

Echoes of footsteps, pulses of life,
Amidst the chaos, joy and strife.
Streets alive with shadows dance,
In heartbeat rush and happenstance.

Each window shines with stories held,
Of laughter, loss, of futures spelled.
Silvery threads connect the ground,
In every corner, life is found.

As day turns night, stars start to glow,
Cities of light beneath the flow.
In the heart of concrete, dreams take flight,
Silvery skylines, a breathtaking sight.

The Song of Windows

Framed glimpses of a world outside,
Through tempered glass, hearts confide.
Each pane a portal, a silent take,
The song of life in the moves we make.

Sunrise spills through gold and green,
Curtains whisper where souls have been.
Voices layer in translucent frames,
Windows shift with joy and pains.

Rain's gentle patter on rooftops sings,
A melody of simple things.
Reflecting warmth, it catches light,
In every window, stories ignite.

At dusk, they glow like fireflies bright,
Harboring moments in gentle night.
The song of windows shall not end,
As life unfolds, and hearts transcend.

Rhythm of the Roofs

In the city, echoes hum,
Tiled tops like dancers come.
Cobbled paths beneath them sway,
Silent steps in bright array.

Chimneys stretch to kiss the sky,
Waves of shingles painted high.
Gables form a symphony,
Nature's tune, a harmony.

Layers stacked in sunlit grace,
Each a story, time's embrace.
Wind whispers through rafters bold,
Secrets of the past retold.

Underneath the moon's soft glow,
Roofs unite, a soft tableau.
Crafted dreams above our heads,
Where the silent spirit treads.

Woven in Bricks

Brick by brick, the story starts,
Laid with care, built with hearts.
Rough and smooth, the textures blend,
Each small piece, a voice, a friend.

Colors merge in earthen ties,
Patterns rise, as old time flies.
Mortar binds the tales we share,
Layered whispers fill the air.

From the ground, they reach the sky,
Hopes and dreams, they stand up high.
Lines of strength in unity,
Every brick a memory.

In the glow of sunset's light,
Walls reflect the day to night.
Woven tales in bricks of clay,
Time's embrace won't fade away.

Patterns in Perspective

Shapes emerge in brighter hues,
Shifting lines, a dance of views.
Angles meet in thoughtful gaze,
Life unfolds in endless maze.

Through the lens, the world expands,
Curved horizons trace our hands.
Every moment framed with care,
Patterns woven, truth laid bare.

Focus shifts, a casual glance,
Within the chaos, find the chance.
Chaos holds a subtle art,
Each new take can play its part.

In the shadows, secrets find,
Depths of beauty intertwined.
Voices echo, soft yet loud,
Art resides among the crowd.

Fluidity of Form

Water flows, a gentle stream,
Dancing light, a sparkling dream.
Curves and bends, an endless play,
Nature's breath in soft ballet.

Silk and stone, a soft embrace,
Motion found in nature's grace.
Ripples tell the tales of time,
Melodies in each soft chime.

Always shifting, never still,
Wind and wave, they bend to thrill.
Form begins to fade and flow,
In this dance, all truths will show.

On the surface, life anew,
Fluid shapes in every hue.
Every drop a story spun,
In this dance, we're always one.

The Pulse of Place

In the heart of town, beats a drum,
Echoes of laughter, a welcoming hum.
Trees sway gently, whispers on air,
Each corner alive, stories to share.

The sun sets low, casting warm hues,
Children at play, in joyous muse.
Bricks and mortar hold secrets tight,
In the pulse of place, day turns to night.

Footsteps retrace where memories lie,
Moments captured beneath the sky.
The rhythm of life in every street,
Unique with each heartbeat, a life so sweet.

Connections blossom, intertwined fate,
In the pulse of place, we all relate.
Nature and urban, a dance in time,
Here, every heartbeat feels like a rhyme.

Vibration in Veneer

Beneath the surface, a tremor waits,
Echo of feelings, as fate dictates.
Walls adorned with shades of truth,
Masking the stories of fleeting youth.

The gloss may shine, but cracks reveal,
Layers of longing that time can't heal.
Hushed tones linger, in corners concealed,
Vibrations of lives, quietly revealed.

Textures tell tales, both rough and fine,
In every crevice, a life aligns.
Veils of the past intertwined with now,
In vibration's pulse, we breathe and bow.

Each whisper soft, yet boldly grand,
In the veneer's glow, our fates expand.
Together we live, under the skin,
Finding the strength to begin again.

Pathways of Perception

Winding roads that twist and turn,
Each step forward, a lesson learned.
Eyes wide open, we seek to know,
In pathways of thought, we ebb and flow.

Landscapes shift with the change of light,
Thoughts intertwine, dark and bright.
Perception's lens shapes how we see,
In the dance of minds, we find the key.

Through shadows cast, we bravely roam,
Finding in difference, we create home.
Guided by stars or the sun's embrace,
Pathways weave tales in time and space.

Every journey leads to hidden sights,
In exploration, we reach new heights.
Together we walk, hand in hand,
In pathways of perception, we understand.

Walls That Sing

Under the arch of the ancient stone,
Echoes of laughter, feelings grown.
Brush of a breeze ignites a tune,
Walls that sing by the light of the moon.

Each crack and crevice holds a song,
Melodies thriving, where we belong.
Windows wide, hearts open wide,
In the gentle waves, we no longer hide.

Chords of memory, a symphony pure,
Notes that linger, warm and sure.
In the dance of shadows, the walls reveal,
Stories of love, hearts they heal.

With every dusk, their voices rise,
In the silence, hope never dies.
Together we listen, to what they bring,
In every heartbeat, the walls that sing.

Nature's Notes in Design

Leaves dance softly in the breeze,
Whispers of the ancient trees.
Water ripples, glimmers bright,
Nature's canvas, pure delight.

Mountains rise against the sky,
Where eagles soar and shadows lie.
Streams weave stories, old and true,
In the heart of vibrant hue.

Petals open, colors blend,
Life's sweet symphony, never end.
Sunsets paint the world with grace,
Every moment, a warm embrace.

Stars begin their nightly show,
Calling dreams from below.
Nature's notes, a soft design,
In every breath, a sacred sign.

The Language of Lines

Lines of horizon stretch afar,
Marking where earth meets star.
Paths that wander, twist, and glide,
Stories drawn with every stride.

Curves of rivers, gentle flow,
Memory trails where echoes grow.
Silhouettes against the night,
Shapes of dreams in quiet light.

Edges sharp or seamlessly blend,
With every turn, new paths ascend.
Between the gaps, mysteries dwell,
In each outline, a tale to tell.

Sketches made with heart and hand,
In every line, a whispered land.
The language spoken, soft and clear,
Guiding us through far and near.

The Architecture of Solitude

In empty rooms, the silence sings,
Echoed thoughts, the mind takes wings.
Walls of stillness, softly penned,
A refuge where the heart can mend.

Shadows play on wooden floors,
Secrets linger behind closed doors.
Light filters through, a golden thread,
Weaving comfort where hope is fed.

Chairs await and tables stand,
Holding stories, hand in hand.
In the quiet, wisdom grows,
In solitude, peace softly flows.

Fleeting moments, softly caught,
In the architect of thought.
A space to dream, a place to be,
In solitude, we find the key.

Spirals in the Skyline

Clouds swirl gently, shapes unclear,
Whispering secrets as they veer.
Tall towers rise, a dance of steel,
In the skyline, dreams conceal.

Streets twist, a labyrinth unfolds,
Stories held in bricks, retold.
Neon lights, a riot of color,
In the city, hearts discover.

Cycles of life, rhythm divine,
In every corner, stars align.
Winding paths, an endless chase,
In spirals, we find our place.

Above the noise, a quiet grace,
In the skyline's vast embrace.
Through every turn, the journey flows,
In these spirals, the spirit grows.

Columns of Time

Ancient stones whisper tales,
Of victories and silent wails.
They stand tall, through storms and sun,
Holding history, one by one.

Each crack a story, carved in grace,
A silent witness to time's embrace.
Moments captured, shadows cast,
In the echoes of the past.

Seasons change, yet they remain,
Guardians of joy, grief, and pain.
In their shade, we pause to dream,
Columns of time, a flowing stream.

Beneath the weight of years gone by,
They reach up, touching the sky.
A bridge of ages, standing firm,
In their strength, we find the term.

Frames of Reflection

In the glass, a world appears,
Caught in laughter, held in tears.
Moments frozen, time held still,
Each frame a dream, a whispered thrill.

Light dances softly on the edge,
Casting thoughts like a sacred pledge.
With every glance, a memory flows,
In quiet corners, the heart knows.

Mirrored thoughts, both bright and dim,
Echoes of a life within.
A tapestry of what we see,
Frames of reflection, setting free.

Captured fragments of who we are,
Guiding us like a distant star.
In each reflection, truth aligned,
Frames of our lives, gently defined.

A Symphony of Steel

Cold metal breaths in the night,
Rings and echoes blend in flight.
Forging paths through dusk and dawn,
In a rhythm that feels like a song.

Wires hum and gears collide,
In the heart, a furnace wide.
Craftsmanship sings in every beat,
A symphony of steel, raw and sweet.

Against the clang, the sparks ignite,
Illuminating shadows in flight.
A dance of creation, bold and real,
Where strength meets art, we feel the wheel.

In the workshop, a vision flows,
As the pulse of the steelwork goes.
Mighty forces in harmony played,
A symphony of steel, proudly displayed.

Lanterns of Design

Crafted wonders, glowing bright,
Lanterns guide us through the night.
Shapes and colors, art defined,
Illuminating paths entwined.

With every flicker, stories bloom,
Casting warmth, dispelling gloom.
Intricate patterns, light's embrace,
Lanterns glow, time leaves its trace.

In chambers hushed, they softly sway,
Drawing dreams as shadows play.
Each design a whisper, a spark,
Guiding souls through the dark.

Brilliance unfolds in twilight's gleam,
Awakening hearts, igniting dreams.
In their light, we find our sign,
Lanterns of design, forever shine.

The Structure of Sound

In whispers soft, the echoes play,
Notes dance lightly, drift away.
Harmony swells in gentle air,
A tapestry rich, woven with care.

Frequencies blend, a vibrant hue,
Each tone a story, bold and true.
Resonance builds, a swell of might,
In the silence, the heart takes flight.

The pulse of life in every beat,
Subtle murmurs, a rhythm sweet.
Chords entwine, a sacred thread,
In the symphony, our dreams are fed.

A world alive with every sound,
In melody's arms, we are bound.
Listen close, let it surround,
In the music, our joys abound.

Weaving in the Wind

A thread of air on a sunny day,
Carries whispers, light as a sway.
Leaves flutter, dance with finesse,
Nature's loom, a soft caress.

Clouds drift by, a tapestry white,
Stitching stories both day and night.
The breeze hums low, a quiet song,
Guiding dreams where they belong.

Vines entwine, embrace the trees,
Songs of the wild on a gentle breeze.
Nature's hands weave, ever so grand,
Creating places where hearts can stand.

In shadows cast by the setting sun,
The fabric of life has just begun.
Weaving moments, soft and blurred,
In every gust, our spirits stirred.

Whims of the Walled

In shadows deep, the secrets keep,
Walls of history, strong and steep.
Whispers float on the evening breeze,
Echoes trapped among the trees.

A glance beyond, a world so wide,
Yet within these walls, dreams abide.
Flickers of light through cracks so small,
Imagination dances in the hall.

Stories linger in quiet sighs,
Soft are the truths in the muted cries.
Bound yet free, the heart does roam,
Finding pathways to call its home.

A paradox of safety, fear,
In every stone, a tale appears.
Walled in, yet longing to explore,
The whims of the heart, forever soar.

The Rhythm of Reflections

In still waters, the world unfolds,
Mirrors whisper, secrets told.
Ripples break the perfect glass,
Time stands still, as moments pass.

Each glance catches the light of day,
Framing memories that drift away.
Shadows dance with a gentle grace,
In every turn, a hidden place.

Echoes linger where silence reigns,
In the depth, life's beauty gains.
Reflections spark in twilight's glow,
A rhythm found in the ebb and flow.

Look within to the depths of night,
In quiet waters, discover light.
The heart's reflection, pure and true,
In every wave, a piece of you.

Blueprints of Silence

In quiet corners where shadows dwell,
The whispers of dreams weave a tale to tell.
Blueprints of silence drawn on the floor,
Echoes of wishes, yearning for more.

Foundations of thoughts resting deep in the night,
Framed by the stars, a glowing delight.
Through stillness we wander, our minds set to roam,
Crafting the blueprints to call them our home.

Structures of Harmony

In every heartbeat, a rhythm is found,
A melody rises, soft and profound.
Structures of harmony, built on the air,
Songs played in silence, beyond all compare.

With every note, the universe sighs,
Tuning our spirits to echo the skies.
We dance in the layers of sounds yet unheard,
Creating connections, where hearts are stirred.

The Symphony of Columns

Columns like pillars hold stories untold,
In their sturdy embrace, our memories fold.
A symphony rises, both strong and divine,
Crafted from echoes, a language in line.

Each step we take echoes against stone,
A heartbeat of heritage, never alone.
Together we stand, through whispers and breath,
Building a legacy that conquers death.

Echoes in the Skylines

In vibrant hues, the city awakes,
Echoes in skylines, the rhythm it makes.
Steel and glass reach for dreams so high,
Stories of travelers woven in the sky.

Amidst the hustle, a moment to pause,
Each skyline a canvas, with its own cause.
From dawn to dusk, the echoes unfold,
A tapestry crafted in colors so bold.

Echoes Through Aisles

Whispers linger in the air,
Softly dancing, unaware.
Footsteps trace a silent song,
Carried where the shadows throng.

Old books stacked in faded rows,
Secrets hid where nobody goes.
Pages flutter, time stands still,
As echoes weave through every thrill.

Memories of laughter and tears,
You can feel the passing years.
Through each aisle, a story glows,
Written where the silence flows.

In this space, the heart will find,
Every treasure left behind.
An endless tale, an open door,
Echoes through the aisles implore.

Riffs in Railing

Worn wood creaks under my weight,
A melody as twilight waits.
Each step brings its own refrain,
Riffs that dance with joy and pain.

Rusty nails in heartbeats sway,
Glimmers of a bright ballet.
Every curve and twist defines,
The music of these aged lines.

Fingers trace the weathered grain,
Drawing forth each lost refrain.
In the stillness, echoes play,
Riffs in metal memories stay.

Beneath the stars' electric glow,
The railing sings of long ago.
A song of life, a sweet embrace,
A melody we can't erase.

The Beat of the Breeze

Gentle whispers through the trees,
Nature's heart beats in the breeze.
Rustling leaves begin to sway,
A rhythm found in night and day.

Sunlight dapples on the ground,
In every moment, life is found.
Soft caresses on the skin,
A song that pulls the soul within.

Winds of change will come and go,
Marking time, their ebb and flow.
In the stillness, listen close,
The breeze reveals what matters most.

Moments captured in the air,
A melody beyond compare.
With every breath, we can believe,
In the magic that we weave.

Sculpture Beneath Skylines

Crafted dreams rise to embrace,
Steel and stone hold time and space.
Each angle tells a tale so bold,
In shadows where the light turns gold.

Figures stand in silent grace,
Stories etched in every place.
An artist's vision, pure and bright,
Reaching far beyond the night.

Footsteps echo, visitors roam,
In this gallery, we find home.
Underneath the vast expanse,
Every glance begins to dance.

So let the skyline frame our dreams,
In sculpture's gaze, our spirit gleams.
A world of shapes, of hopes combined,
Beneath the stars, our hearts aligned.

Frames of Light and Shadow

In whispered corners, secrets play,
Chasing shadows at the end of day.
Golden beams through branches weep,
Painting memories we wish to keep.

Framed in twilight, glimmers glow,
Echoes of laughter, soft and slow.
Every flicker tells a tale,
In this dance of light, we sail.

Against the dark, the colors bloom,
Illuminating every room.
With each step, a story unfolds,
In frames of light, the heart beholds.

The mind drifts where the shadows rest,
In the interplay, we're truly blessed.
Caught between the dusk and dawn,
In the frames of dusk, we're drawn.

The Harmony of Heights

Where rugged peaks embrace the sky,
The wind whispers gently by.
Each summit holds a promise clear,
Of dreams that rise, of hopes that steer.

In valleys deep, the echoes sing,
The beauty found in every spring.
High above, the eagles soar,
In harmony, we yearn for more.

With every climb, the spirit wakes,
Scaling heights, our courage shakes.
The vast expanse, a canvas bright,
In heights of harmony, we find our light.

Among the clouds, we dance and twirl,
In nature's rhythm, our hearts unfurl.
The harmony of heights we seek,
In every breath, we feel so weak.

Breath of the Building

In the stillness, walls breathe deep,
Stories of those who chose to leap.
Each brick a whisper, a soft sigh,
Echoes of laughter that never die.

Windows wide, the light cascades,
Casting shadows where memory fades.
Laughter dances down the halls,
In every corner, history calls.

From rooftops high to basement low,
The spirit of life continues to flow.
With every heartbeat, the structure hums,
In breaths of the building, life becomes.

And as the seasons gently shift,
The breath of the past gives us a gift.
Each echo a reminder, strong and clear,
In the breath of the building, we feel near.

Mosaic of Moments

Fragments of time, a patchwork bright,
Each moment, a spark that ignites.
Colors collide in joyful refrain,
Woven together in laughter and pain.

Stitched by hands that care to hold,
A tapestry rich, not bought or sold.
In each corner, a story rests,
Moments captured, life's true guests.

From whispers lost to joyful shouts,
The mosaic of life holds troubles and doubts.
Yet in the chaos, beauty is found,
In every heartbeat, love is profound.

So gather the pieces, let them align,
In this mosaic, let our hearts twine.
Every moment a thread, interlace,
In the fabric of life, we find our place.

Whispers of the Walls

In silent rooms where secrets dwell,
Each brick and creak has tales to tell.
Shadows dance in muted light,
Echoes hide in folds of night.

Faint whispers drift on dusty air,
Memories linger, soft and rare.
Paint peels gently, stories unfold,
Of laughter lost and love grown cold.

Windows gaze with patient eyes,
Witness to the world's goodbyes.
Each corner cradles sorrow's sigh,
While hopes are born and dreams do fly.

In these walls, life's tapestry,
Woven with threads of history.
Listen close, for they reveal,
The heart's deep truth, the soul's appeal.

The Geometry of Dreams

Shapes collide in mind's embrace,
Angles twist in thoughts' soft space.
Circles spin like midnight's grace,
While time dissolves, a fleeting trace.

Lines intersect, a fate entwined,
Each vertex holds a dream refined.
Parallels may never meet,
Yet hope persists, a rhythm sweet.

Within the frame of starry night,
Figures dance in pure delight.
The graph of life, with twists and turns,
In silent depths, our passion burns.

Bold perspectives take their flight,
In woven patterns, dark and light.
The geometry of dreams unfolds,
In whispered truths, our future molds.

Crescendo in Concrete

Steel and stone, a rising roar,
Each stride echoes on the floor.
Buildings stretch with timeless might,
A symphony of urban light.

Concrete towers pierce the sky,
Where dreams can soar, and spirits fly.
With every sound, a pulse, a beat,
Life unfolds in rhythm's heat.

Streets are veins that carve the land,
As strangers pass, a silent band.
In every crack, a story hides,
In shadows deep, ambition rides.

A crescendo builds, our lives entwined,
In city's heartbeat, peace we find.
Harmony in chaos swells,
In concrete jungles, magic dwells.

Harmony in Tiles

Colors blend in patterned grace,
Each tile tells its own embrace.
Ceramic dreams beneath our feet,
A mosaic where paths meet.

In kitchens warm, where laughter brews,
The dance of light in vibrant hues.
Stepping stones to cherished days,
In every inch, our love displays.

Patterns whisper in the light,
Stories captured, pure delight.
From every corner, beauty glows,
As time within this space flows.

Harmony crafted, hand in hand,
Tiles unite in life's grand plan.
A symphony of sights and sounds,
In every square, our joy abounds.

Chant of the Cityscape

Amidst the towers, voices rise,
Echoes of dreams fill the skies.
Concrete pulses, can you feel?
Life's a dance, time to reveal.

Streetlamps flicker, shadows play,
Neon lights guide the way.
A symphony of sound and sight,
City's heart beats through the night.

Beneath the bridges, whispers flow,
Tales of the lost, tales we know.
Horns and laughter, a rich refrain,
Each moment captured, joy and pain.

In the alleys, secrets hide,
Dreamers walk with quiet pride.
The city breathes, alive, awake,
In every corner, souls partake.

The Rhythm of Rooflines

Above the streets, rooflines converge,
A dance of angles, a silent urge.
Chimneys stand like sentinels bold,
Guarding stories, memories told.

Tiles of blue, and tiles of grey,
Each a note in the grand ballet.
Skylights gleam, the sun peeks through,
A canvas painted in shades of blue.

Raindrops tap on the ledge above,
Nature's music, a song of love.
The roofs hum softly, shadows blend,
In every corner, life to mend.

As day retreats, stars appear,
An orchestra playing, crystal clear.
Under the rooftops, dreams abide,
In their rhythm, we all confide.

Silence Between the Walls

Walls hold secrets, silent tight,
Echoes linger, out of sight.
Whispers shared, dreams confined,
In stillness, thoughts aligned.

Each crack and crevice tells a tale,
Paths of love or journeys frail.
In the silence, hearts collide,
Within these walls, we cannot hide.

Forgotten memories softly wane,
Laughter lingered, yet leaves a stain.
Silhouettes dance in muted light,
Forming bonds that feel so right.

Stillness breathes between the bricks,
Moments passed, and time transfixed.
Within these frames, we find our peace,
In silent spaces, souls release.

Vibrations in the Vault

Vaulted ceilings, echoes loom,
Chambers rich with thoughts that bloom.
In the stillness, whispers glide,
Notes of longing, hearts collide.

The air vibrates with ancient tales,
Of love that triumphs, never fails.
Beneath the arches, hope takes flight,
Guided by stars that fill the night.

Frequencies dance, a cosmic thread,
Linking lives that once were wed.
In the vault's embrace, we find our way,
Stirring dreams by night and day.

Resonating, the past is near,
Harmonies whisper, crystal clear.
Within this space, we come alive,
In every heartbeat, we truly thrive.

Silhouettes at Dusk

Shadows stretch across the ground,
Whispers fill the air around.
Figures dance in fading light,
Nature sighs, day turns to night.

Colors blend in soft embrace,
Time slows down, a slower pace.
Stars begin to twinkle bright,
Guiding dreams with gentle light.

The horizon whispers low,
Secrets only dusk can show.
Each silhouette tells a tale,
Echoes of the day unveil.

Underneath the twilight sky,
Softly breathe a gentle sigh.
In the hush of evening's grace,
Find your heart, find your place.

Arches of Expression

In vibrant hues, emotions rise,
Beneath the arches of the skies.
Brushes dance with fervent glee,
Crafting worlds for all to see.

Whispers of the heart take flight,
In strokes of passion, pure delight.
Every line, a story spun,
In the glow of the setting sun.

Captured moments painted well,
Echoes of a timeless spell.
Art unfolds in every glance,
Inviting souls to join the dance.

Beneath the arches, dreams arise,
In vibrant colors, life complies.
Expression flows, an endless stream,
Awakening each hidden dream.

Chords of the City

In alleys where the echoes roam,
City beats, a vibrant home.
Voices mingle, tales untold,
Rhythms of the brave and bold.

Neon lights like stars ignite,
Guiding wanderers through the night.
Every corner, every street,
Plays a song, a pulse, a beat.

The skyscrapers touch the shade,
In the twilight, dreams are made.
Chords of laughter, love, and life,
Resonate through joy and strife.

Invitations in the air,
Promises that linger there.
In the city's heart, we find,
A symphony that moves the mind.

The Blueprint of Silence

In quiet moments, thoughts take flight,
Sketches of dreams in the still of night.
Silence whispers secrets deep,
In the peace where echoes sleep.

Pages bare, yet filled with grace,
Every line a sacred space.
Plans are drawn, intentions clear,
In the quiet, we hold dear.

Dreams await the hands of time,
Blueprints crafted in silence prime.
The heart's design, a fragile thread,
Weaving futures yet unsaid.

In every pause, a chance to see,
The world unfolds, a mystery.
In whispered thoughts, we come alive,
In silence, our hopes survive.

Harmony Beyond the Horizon

In skies where colors blend and play,
The sun bids night a soft goodbye.
Waves whisper secrets, come what may,
Together they dance, under the sky.

Mountains stand tall, embracing the light,
Their shadows stretch, a calming grace.
Nature's chorus sings through the night,
Finding our peace in this vast space.

Stars twinkle gently, a celestial glow,
Guiding lost souls, their paths unwind.
In dreams of unity, love starts to grow,
A symphony crafted, entwined and aligned.

So let us wander where harmony calls,
Hand in hand, with open hearts.
For beyond the horizon, where beauty enthralls,
Is where our forever truly starts.

Timeless Symmetries

In every petal, a story spins,
A dance of patterns, a world so grand.
Life's canvas woven, where beauty begins,
With echoing echoes of a master's hand.

Each breath is measured, in nature's song,
The heartbeat of Earth, steady and true.
In spirals and curves, we all belong,
Timeless symmetries, deep within you.

Through seasons dancing, we find our way,
The balance of night and the blush of morn.
In the fold of petals, where dreams will stay,
Timeless symmetries are lovingly born.

Let us celebrate the lines intertwined,
As we walk through the garden of fate.
In every heartbeat, a truth defined,
Timeless symmetries lead us to create.

Structures of Serenity

In gentle arches where shadows wane,
Quiet corners whisper of peace.
Time flows softly like summer rain,
In structures of serenity, all fears cease.

Brick by brick, a refuge is built,
Each moment collected, each memory cherished.
In spaces adorned with calm and quilt,
The worries of yesterday slowly perish.

Light filters softly through glass and stone,
Casting patterns of joy on the ground.
In every nook, we feel less alone,
In structures of serenity, comfort is found.

So let us gather in this sacred place,
Where laughter echoes and love grows wide.
In the heart of stillness, we find our grace,
In structures of serenity, our souls abide.

Echoes in the Stone

Deep in the earth, stories unfold,
Whispers of ages, wisdom unspun.
In every crack, a memory told,
Echoes in the stone, where time has run.

Mountains hold secrets, shadows embrace,
History woven in layers of gray.
Silent observers of the human race,
Echoes in the stone, a timeless ballet.

Caves hum softly, with voices from past,
Carved by the rivers, shaped by the tide.
In stillness, their messages hold steadfast,
Echoes in the stone, in nature we bide.

Let us listen close, to the earth's gentle song,
For wisdom rests deeply, in each weathered face.
In echoes of stone, we truly belong,
A connection profound, in this sacred space.

Vitality in Verticals

In steel and glass, we rise and thrive,
Each floor a dream, alive, alive.
Vertical whispers, ambition's song,
Reaching upward, where we belong.

Sunlight dances on concrete bright,
Casting shadows, a playful sight.
Through windows wide, perspectives shift,
Life's heartbeat in each daring lift.

Spirits soar in the city air,
Climbing heights, we dare to care.
With every step, new visions bloom,
In this vertical space, we find our room.

Cadence of Cornices

Beneath the arch of crafted stone,
Cornices whisper tales unknown.
Rhythms drawn from ages past,
In every line, memories cast.

Gentle curves, a graceful sway,
Holding history in the clay.
Where beauty meets where time persists,
In solid forms, the artist's tryst.

From city blocks to country lanes,
Each cornice holds the joys and pains.
A silent guard of dreams once shared,
In every ridge, a hope declared.

Frames of Freedom

Fences thin, yet hearts expand,
In every frame, we take a stand.
Open vistas, horizons wide,
In colors bold, our dreams abide.

Windows look out; walls hold in,
Within each frame, new worlds begin.
Painted skies and swirling thoughts,
In every glance, a lesson sought.

With every border, we redefine,
What it means to truly shine.
Boundless realms in confined space,
Within these frames, we find our place.

The Art of Elevation

Ascending paths of shifting light,
Each step we take, a dance of height.
With every breath, the air grows thin,
In the art of rise, we're born within.

The mountain's call, the skyline's lure,
Through struggle fierce, we find the cure.
Elevate thoughts, ascend the soul,
In heights achieved, we find our goal.

Above the clouds, the world unfurls,
In the quiet, a new vision swirls.
To elevate is to embrace,
The purest form of life's sweet grace.

Geometric Whispers

Shapes that dance in silent light,
Angles sharp, a poet's sight.
Lines converge, a hidden thread,
In this space, thoughts are wed.

Circles turn with gentle grace,
Each curve draws a sacred space.
Triangles form a sturdy base,
In whispers, we find our place.

Patterns in Stone

Rocks unveil their ancient tales,
In every crease, history sails.
Textures worn by time's caress,
Nature's art, we must confess.

Layers formed in quiet strife,
Echoes of primordial life.
From the mountain to the sea,
Patterns speak in harmony.

Cadence of Beams

Sunlight spills through branches wide,
Golden beams where shadows hide.
In the woods, the echoes play,
A symphony of light and sway.

Each flicker tells a fleeting tale,
As the whispers softly sail.
Nature's rhythm, pulse so true,
Guides the heart, it beckons you.

Lines that Sing

In pencil strokes and vibrant hues,
Artisans craft their silent muse.
Graphite flows with passion's might,
Like melodies that take to flight.

Each line a note, a sweet refrain,
Whispers echo through the grain.
Together form a joyous song,
In their embrace, we all belong.

Essence in Edifices

Mighty towers touch the sky,
Stone and glass, they reach up high.
Within their walls, stories unfold,
Whispers of dreams, both new and old.

Silhouettes against the dawn,
Silent echoes, life moves on.
Foundations strong, yet hearts are light,
In each structure, a guiding light.

Windows frame a world so bright,
Each moment held, in sheer delight.
Inside, the warmth of love abides,
In edifices, life resides.

Above the chaos, calm is found,
In the spaces that surround.
The essence of who we aspire,
In brick and beam, ignites desire.

Crescendo of Clay

Hands mold the earth, soft and warm,
Crafting shapes, a silent charm.
Fingers dance, a rhythm flows,
In each curve, the spirit grows.

A wheel spins fast, the clay takes flight,
Artistry blooms, a pure delight.
From flat to round, a vessel born,
In the dance of creation, each is adorned.

Colors burst in vibrant hues,
Under the glaze, a hidden muse.
Each piece tells a tale divine,
In the crescendo, hearts entwine.

Fire's embrace, transformation true,
In the kiln, dreams come to view.
From earth to art, a journey shared,
In each creation, love declared.

Fluid Forms

Gentle waves upon the shore,
Whispers of a sea's old lore.
Liquid dances, free and bold,
In fluid forms, the stories told.

Colors mingle, sway and glide,
Painting visions, side by side.
Each drop a moment, fleeting fast,
In shimmering ripples, memories cast.

Beneath the surface, secrets lie,
Depths unknown, beneath the sky.
The fabric of time, woven tight,
In fluid forms, both dark and light.

Emotions flow, a current strong,
In water's embrace, we all belong.
With each tide, a journey begun,
In the dance of the many, we become one.

Harmony in Heights

Mountain peaks in soft embrace,
Nature's canvas, vastspace.
Echoes call from rocky heights,
In harmony, the spirit ignites.

Through winding paths, the journey waits,
Each step taken, the heart resonates.
Crimson hues in sunset's view,
A symphony of the brave and true.

Chirping birds in morning's glow,
A chorus sings, the world below.
In nature's arms, we find our place,
In heights where dreams embrace grace.

The stars above, a guiding choir,
In the stillness, our souls aspire.
With every breath, we feel the way,
In harmony, we find our stay.

The Narrative of Nooks

In quiet corners, secrets dwell,
Whispers echo, stories swell.
A worn-out book, a faded light,
The world outside fades from sight.

In shadows cast by gentle night,
Dreams take flight in soft twilight.
Every nook a tale to tell,
Hidden wonders, hearts compel.

A chipping chair, a tapestry,
Threads connect our history.
In silence, memories converge,
Life's soft narratives emerge.

Beneath the stars, in stillness found,
Hidden spaces, love unbound.
In every nook, a spark ignites,
In the dark, pure joy ignites.

Dimensions of Delight

In playful laughter, moments rise,
Bright colors dance, ignite the skies.
With every smile, the heart takes flight,
In every glance, a burst of light.

Through fields of roses, joy is spread,
In simple pleasures, we are led.
A warm embrace, a gentle touch,
In small things, we find so much.

Together we weave our bright dreams,
In laughter, love, and joyful streams.
The world transforms in shades of glee,
In every note, we truly see.

As daylight fades, the stars ignite,
In every heart, a spark of light.
Dimensions wide, our spirits soar,
In every moment, we adore.

Milton Keynes UK
Ingram Content Group UK Ltd.
UKHW032036191024
449814UK00010B/469